THE HIDDEN MONSTER: PEDOPHILIA

By

Shawn Michael Dove

ISBN: 1-4033-8061-9 (Electronic)
ISBN: 1-4033-8062-7 (Softcover)

Library of Congress Control Number: 2002095514

This book is printed on acid free paper.

Printe in the United States of America
Bloomington, IN

1stBooks – rev. 10/23/02

TABLE OF CONTENTS

INTRODUCTION

PEDOPHILIA: THE HIDDEN MONSTER

P-E-D-O-P-H-I-L-I-A...P-E-D-O-P-H-I-L-E...the very words bring up anger, rage, hatred, resentments, pain, and hurt. Even horrid, debilitating nightmares that have rattled many precious lives for years, for generations, will come forward.

WHY???? How can some one be so hated, and at one time so loved??

How could this devastation go on for so long and little is known about this horrific, devastating behavior???

How can a person reap so much havoc in another human being, an entire family, and continue on with the destruction of others??????

Why is this sickness so hard to detect???

Why don't more victims of pedophiles come forward, so this hell can stop, and the victims get the treatment that they need???

This book will not answer all of the questions about pedophilia; that will only be done in time, further study, and further healing of the victims, and the pedophiles. This will be a double-edged process, a paradoxical phenomenon that will bring light to this hellish behavior, and healings to most all concerned.

This subject matter is very sensitive and will touch the hearts of many people. This book is to help shed more light on a monster that we all have tried to shove into a closet and have tried to forget. Only to have this monster raise it's savage head in more of our lives; and for eternity in the victims.

The secrecy, cover-up, denial, power and control all that are in darkness must be brought to light. This monster has had control over many lives and some religious institutions for way to long; the victims are slowly coming forth with their devastating nightmares of hell and torment. The nightmares of these monstrous things that have happened some 5, 10, 15, maybe 20+ years ago are still affecting their very lives today.

The more and more this monster is kept in the darkness, the more lives that will continue to be consumed by the beast.

Knowledge is power, and one of the combatants against pedophilia.

Victims sharing their devastation and pain is the beginning of the long healing process they will soon choose to go through.

Ignorance is no excuse; continual devastation of young lives for generations, can not be tolerated; the only hope is more knowledge, more study, more listening to the precious victims, and help for the victims, their families, and also the pedophiles as well.

Together let's begin to understand the monster within these people, so one day we have ***"NO MORE VICTIMS"***...

As you read this book you may or may not agree with a lot of the information within, the idea is that this is some information that needs to be known so more of the healing process can soon begin.

The days of keeping this monster in the closet is over; all that has done is reaped more victims, and devastated more lives. Knowledge is power and it is time to seize this power and to start or to continue their healing process.

The war against pedophilia has already begun; the fight to learn all will be the intelligence reports so we will know where to find the enemy and how to defeat the enemy in the days ahead. WE WILL WIN!!!!

PART I

PEDOPHILIA:

THE HIDDEN MONSTER WITHIN

For decades this monster has been shoved down deep into the closets of our society. Our very culture has been riddled with secrecy, denial, betrayal, and cover-up. One of the ways to get through this hideous devastation is to deny that it ever happened, tell the victim to forget it, and life went on as before. The predator may no longer be around the victim, but the hell and anguish will be with the victim forever.

Things like this don't happen, it's not conceivable that an adult would have or even try to have sex with a child, well enough alone to rape/molest them. All of this must be in the child's imagination, "I know that person and there is

1

no way that this God Fearing person could ever think of doing anything like that." "The CHILD is sick, the CHILD must be trying to get even with that person for some reason."

Most responses used to be mostly against the child, as if the child is lying, it was all the child's fault, and the child was forced to keep the morbid secret to their selves.

If only the adults would listened to the truth and really started to learn about this monster back then…

If the problem never happened, if the problem never existed why does anyone need to learn anything, right????

Many years' later, countless, precious victims later, for the most part there is the "Out Of Sight, Out Of Mind" mentality still in usage today.

Why all the cover-up??? Why all the denial??? Why aren't more people listening to the poor victims, why aren't more people standing up for them???

If a child comes to a responsible adult and shares with this person of things that is happening to them and they don't understand why, chances are 99% sure that this child is truly being raped and the authorities need to know about this horrid behavior that has happened to this child. The child needs to be reassured that they are doing the right thing and that things will be checked out, that people care for them and want these bad things to stop so the child can get help.

In most cases the above doesn't happen, the child is the one that gets ridiculed, and will go through more mental, and verbal abuse by more adults.

Which leads us to today:

If none of these things were going on before why is there more and more victims coming forth sharing more and more of their years of hell, torment and pain?

Why is one of the most prestigious religious organizations so embroiled in one of the most tragic cover-ups in their entire history???

Why just the very words pedophilia—pedophiles—child molesters send anger and rage through so many people?

Knowledge is power, knowledge is strength, knowledge is empowering; now is the time to learn all that one can about this hidden monster that can lurk inside a person and stay hidden, even after they have lashed out and raped.

When a child or now an adult say that they have been raped, things need to be turned over to the authorities to be investigated. The life you might save from further years of hellish nightmares might be someone that you love.

CHAPTER I

PEDOPHILIA

PEDOPHILIA: **Is a psychological, personality disorder, which is learned. A person may believe that they have an uncontrollable, fixated desire, a compulsion to have sex with children. This person will go too great lengths to temporary satisfy these desires.**

Pedophilia is not something that is new, and that has just sprung up in the last few years. I'm sure that pedophilia can he traced all the ways back to Biblical Days. Pedophilia, like so many things we don't understand and that is so horrific for one to imagine, we have a tendency to

5

want to shove it into a closet, slam and lock the door, then hoping and praying that this monster will go away. We also know that the monster will not go away, and that something must be done.

Some research that has been done says: That one out of three girls will be raped/molested by their 18th birthday. One out of six boys are raped/molested by their 18th birthday. These are the results of trying to keep this monster in the closet!!!!!!

"WHAT'S DONE IN DARKNESS MUST BE BROUGHT TO LIGHT"!!!!!!

When a child, maybe now an adult, comes forward and begins to share their horrific abuse, chances are very high that these events did happen, and a further investigation needs to begin. The victim needs to be able to tell of the events openly and honestly, as things happened, not lead, not manipulated by the investigators. The dates and times may be off, but the places and things that actually happened need to be paid attention to.

Keeping in mind that the potential victim has gone through pure hell, they have been through a psychological nightmare, for years on end. The potential victim may think that all these terrible things that have happened to them was their entire fault. (They may have been told that by the pedophile). The potential victim may have been told so many times that all of these things that were happening were not bad things like in the newspapers and on TV, that this is a way this pedophile is showing how much that they love the child. The child wanting to believe this soon does, if for nothing else but to hold on to their sanity. This doesn't take away the hell that this potential victim will be going through.

If the potential victim doesn't tell a responsible adult soon, they will soon begin any of many coping skills to stay alive. This has to be a very helpless, a very scary position for anyone to be in, especially a child...

The victim may have tried to tell an adult of what is happening to them and this person (s) didn't believe or want to believe the child. This person made excuses for the things that maybe happening, or just out right told the child that THEY were lying, that this person knows this adult and there is no way that these things were happening to them; or the child is accused of bringing all of this on themselves and it was their fault that anything had happened, IF anything did happen at all.

Being told that these things are not happening to them, or that all of these things are THEIR FAULT, by this person (s) is as devastating to the child then the actual abuses.

These allegations need to be checked out and investigated; justice must prevail, for the healing process to begin for the victim, the victims' family and the pedophile.

Another devastating happening is, when the pedophile is asked what is going on with this person and this child and the pedophile will lie. It is their word against the child's, now whom would you believe? The pedophile might say that the child is lying; the child didn't understand what was happening. The pedophile will tell any story to clear their self and to get back with the victim and to continue to rape/molest them.

Now the pedophile has something else to hold over the child's head, "See you tried to lie your way through this, they will never believe you now", so the raping and molesting may even increase, and the victim will feel even more out of control, totally helpless, worthless, and confused.

Pedophilia is hard to detect, because if a person doesn't expect an adult being up to something, the behavior of the adult will honestly look like a person that truly cares for and enjoys being around children. The happiness, and joy of the child with the adult and all things surrounding this person seem to be very genuine. That is why it is so hard to detect if anything is going on or not, in these early stages.

One must really know their child and to truly notice any of they're habits or attitudes changing. Then to lovingly ask the child if anything is going on, and to check out their child's friends that they are hanging out with the most.

It's so hard to find the truth when so much is clouded in darkness.

Patients will be the victors, and things will soon come to light.

I must add that there are thousands of people that truly love children and help out thousands of children daily, and are fine up standing people. These people would never harm any child in their care. So if you sense something maybe going on, please handle your inquiry of your child with tender loving care and understanding. There are chances that nothing is going on and there is no reason to alarm your child. All one can do at this point is be supportive, and reassuring that your child can come to you at anytime with any questions about anything that is happening to them that they don't understand.

Once that allegations have been brought against an adult for raping/molesting a child, and lets say that the allegations-nothing is proven, it may be wise to not let the child go back around this individual; it will not be safe for the child. If this person is a pedophile, it will only be a matter of time before it comes to light, this child has been through to much hell already, lets not increase the chances of the child being hurt any more. The sad part is that there will be more victims before this pedophile will get some help.

The very spirit, the very will of the child has been damaged; their innocence has been stolen and taken from them pre-maturely. Their trust, and love in adults can be damaged for life. In some cases the very willingness to live is to great, and some victims do take their lives. No one will believe them (may be their belief), their offender is still running ramped, maybe even raping and hurting more victims, more precious children.

"When will this monster be stopped??????"

"Why doesn't more victims come forward?"

"Why don't more people tell their stories of the hell and torment that they are going through?"

"Why do victims choose to keep this all a secret and not tell anyone about what has and still is happening to them???"

The reasons are so numerous, I'm sure they are near never ending.

Some of the reasons maybe, as mentioned earlier that no one they have told believes them anyway, so why tell anyone else. The victims are so embarrassed to tell anyone about these gross and sickening things that was done to him or her. Some victims may think all that has happened to them was their fault, and that they caused all the things that has happened to them. So why tell??? They may think that they will be the ones in trouble not the one that raped them.

Some of the victims truly believed that the pedophile loved them, and the things that was happening to them was because of that love, so why would they want to get a person in trouble that really loves them.

Maybe the pedophile has told the victim that if they ever tell that the pedophile will be arrested, put in prison forever and they will never be able to see them again. The pedophile may then say that if this happens that this would be the child's fault for telling.

The pedophile may go as far as to physically threaten the victims that if they would ever tell the pedophile will harm/kill a family member or them. The child lives with this on going fear all of their life, because some victims may never tell of their hell tell some decades later.

There is a great deal of responsibility the pedophile will put on the child/victim. These victims need help, guidance, therapy, resolution, and the slow true healing process must begin so the victims can slowly get back to something that resembles a normal peaceful life for them.

So they may become as healthy of a person as they can be, taking into consideration all the hell the victims have been through. Getting them all the help that they need so they, the victim, doesn't become one of the things that they grew to hate the most—a pedophile—themselves.

None of this can be accomplished if this monster is kept in the closet.

Everything that is done in the depths of secrecy, lies and denial must be brought to light.

People must understand that the cover-up and denial of a pedophile is surely not helping that person's victim (s), and it is not helping that pedophile either. The pedophile has a sickness; they have a behavioral disorder that needs intense therapy and help. If that pedophile doesn't get therapy, and in some cases "In Your Face Type Therapy", the chances of them re-offending again are extremely high.

Once a pedophile has been caught, and charges are pressed on this person, this pedophile should not just get slapped on the hands and told to never do this again, and get sent on their ways. Chances are extremely high that after this "fear factor" wears off, this pedophile will be back to molesting and raping children again. This is so sad.

Even though therapy is strongly urged for all pedophiles, therapy is not that magic wand, that magic cure. That pedophile must first want the help; they must truly want to change their sick behavior, before anything will work for them.

This therapy can be mandated for the pedophile, and hopefully one day the pedophile will begin to see some of the devastation that they have caused, and to see the true need to change and to never have any more victims.

So what is known about pedophilia?

As more and more this monster raises it's ugly head; the more and more that the beast pounds on the door; the more and more lives that are devastated by the beast; we are slowly learning more about this monster within. By having more knowledge of this sickness, some of our questions are being answered; these are answers to the questions and not justifications to the devastation, for there is no justification to the devastation that is left behind in the victims of a pedophile.

Pedophilia, in most cases, can be traced all the way back to the pedophile's childhood/teens. Not all children/teens have been raped/molested when they were young, most have been, by a member of their family, a neighbor, teacher, priest, a person that has befriended them, another child, in most cases it is by someone that the child knows, and sad to say—trusts.

Another example is that a child may have grown up in a home where there was extreme physical and mental abuse throughout their childhood. In some cases the child may have been brutally beaten on a number of occasions, may it have been by an adult male or female. The child will slowly begin to build up coping devices to handle this torture that they have to put up with in their lives. Some where in their informative years they have learned that sex is a tool for punishment, or sex is an escape from the hell and torment that they are living in, soon sex becomes a part of their coping devices to stay alive. These children can soon grow into very angry adults, some will chose to act out to vent this pent up anger and rage that they have inside of them.

One more reason, (of many) maybe that a child going through the experimental stages of their life, when experimenting with sex, that they choose to continue to have sex with the same age group throughout their lives, for one reason or another. They may feel more in control, more relaxed then to have sex with a peer or older.

There are numerous reasons why someone has chosen this lifestyle; the important thing is to learn all one can to help the healing process of the victim's, their families, and the pedophile.

NOTE: It is important to say at this time that all people that have been raped/molested when they were children/teens did not turn out to be pedophiles. There have been people that have been through hell in their

childhood and chose to grow up and live the best life they could, considering their past.

I'm sure there are pedophiles that have went through little to no hell in their childhoods and have chosen this lifestyle, because that is what they want to do.

The pedophile is very cunning, conning, manipulative, and premeditative in most that they do. **Pedophilia is a part of this person,** and they have many other good and positive traits in them, which also add to things being so difficult in knowing this person's real motives and intents.

In most cases the pedophile will not just snatch a child from some place, in most cases there will be days, weeks maybe even months of setting the child up for that day that this pedophile will have already planned out in their head, to rape/molest the child.

The pedophile will, in most cases, befriend the child and maybe even some of their friends as well. Slowly the pedophile will gain the child's trust and further work themselves into the child's life. In some cases the pedophile will meet the child's family, even befriending the family as well. Unfortunately, this is all part of the pedophile's "Set Up and Grooming" of not only the potential victim, but also their entire family.

In some cases the pedophile may get financially involved with the family, only to use this against the family at a later date.

When ever the pedophile begins to feel very comfortable with their surroundings, and the family, is when they will slowly begin to want the potential victim alone more often. This is further setting the potential victim up, getting the confidence of the victim, and their family even more.

In some cases, if the pedophile can not have the child when they want the child, the pedophile could get angry, upset and storm away, and the family won't see them for awhile. The pedophile will soon get very jealous of the child, jealous of the child's own family. The pedophile will soon begin to think that the child is theirs, mainly because of all that the pedophile has **invested** in the child.

When the potential victim seems to like, maybe even love the pedophile this is a sign that the pedophile has been looking for all along; the day that the pedophile will rape/molest the child will be near.

By now the family has grown fond of the pedophile, may even consider this person a part of the family. The family has accepted this person as a kind, loving, considerate, fun person to be around, (for the most part, most pedophiles are fun to be around, it's their objective which is devastating), and the family feels quite comfortable having this person around at any time. These are all things that the pedophile looks for in their "Set Up and Grooming" process as well.

The "Acting Out" process is next. These things have been gone over in the pedophile's mind more then once. The pedophile may have the time, place, and everything that they want to happen all lined out in their heads. Even the way they want the child to react and what they would want the child to say. All of this is rehearsed many times in their head.

By now the pedophile may have the child's 100% trust, and the child may even love this person, and will do almost anything that the pedophile will ask of them to do. The Child will trust this person with their life, and the child will want to believe anything that the pedophile tells them. This trust, this unconditional love of this child, this wanting to be loved and accepted so badly by an adult, is all things that the pedophile looks for and preys on all along.

All along the pedophile may be telling the child how special the child is to them, how much the pedophile loves the child, and hopes the child will never leave them, that they are close friends, and friends can and do special things for each other. All of these things will lead to the acting out, the rape/molesting of the child. The child is eating all of this attention up, these are all things that a child loves to hear, and of course the child wants to believe all of these things.

Then the day and the moment are here when the precious child will be a victim.

If for some reason that the child may say "NO!" or begin to resist in any way, the pedophile will verbally use everything in their power to entice, to control, and manipulate the victim to do what they want the child to do. May it be from begging and pleading, to promises of buying them something special that the victim has always wanted, telling the victim how much the pedophile loves them and they want to show the child how much. Telling the child that the pedophile just wants to teach them about sex. That when the child gets older and meets that special someone, that they will know how to keep that person happy. The conning and manipulation during this time is outrageous.

The confusion, the fear, the helplessness, hopelessness, just rips through the victim's being. It's like being stuck in one's nightmare and not knowing how to escape. With all the begging and pleading of the pedophile, the child may be so scared that they will try to run away, when they find out that they can't run, they can't fight this adult, they feel that the only way that they can escape this horror is to give in—most victims do. The experience is so devastating to the child that they will do almost anything to have this nightmare to end.

When things are finished, the pedophile will continue to promise the victim anything to keep the victim from telling on them, from promises of money, to that new bike or to get their bike all fixed up, almost anything to get the victim to be quite and to come back to the pedophile's web. (This is called the "Aftermath").

The pedophile will continue to rape/molest this child until they get tired of them, or until they get caught. When the pedophile gets tired of this victim, then the stalking, the setup and the grooming process of another child will begin.

If for any reason that this victim continues to resist, from time to time, the pedophile will soon set up and groom another potential victim, then sport this new child off in front of the victim in hopes to get that past victim jealous and to come back to the pedophile's web of hell and torment.

If and when the victim ever tells a responsible adult about what hell that they have been going through, the horror, the pain, the debilitating affects can and will shake their very soul. The hell that they have went through up tell that time will continue into the days ahead. All of this hell must be brought to light so the healing process can begin. The victim will need total reassurance that they are doing the right thing for themselves and for any other potential victims that would be as long as this pedophile is running rampant. Also reassuring the victim that they will be safe, there will be people watching over them to help and protect them.

Reassuring the victim that the pedophile needs help, needs therapy, and this is the only way that this person will receive help is by going to prison to get it. Letting the victim know that if this person really loved them that there will be no way that this person could possibly do all the horrid things that they done to them. It's now time to get help for the victim and the pedophile.

As for the victim, the victim needs a good therapy program that will slowly work them through all the hell they have been through, reassuring them that they have done nothing wrong, that they were totally innocent in all of this nightmare, and that they done the right thing by telling of the hell that they have went through.

The pedophile will need therapy as well. The pedophile will need to find out all the whys, when's, and where's of their sickness. The pedophile must truly want to change;

they must truly want the help, or all of the therapy in the world will not help them.

In most cases a pedophile will want to change, maybe in the beginning for no other reason as to not spend the rest of their lives in prison. As the pedophile goes through therapy, most will truly see the hell and havoc that they have caused and develop victim empathy, and truly want to have *"NO MORE VICTIMS"*. There is hope for everyone the pedophile is no exception.

Once a pedophile has done their time, it is strongly advised that they will continue their therapy on the streets. The pedophile must not be around any children and especially none of their past victims.

Once the pedophile is truly doing therapy, the chances of this person re-offending are much less then a person with no therapy at all.

FURTHER AFFECTS

The tragic devastation that follows a pedophile's actions is overwhelming. The ripple effect can touch everyone in that city and beyond. To think of all the people that truly loves this pedophile and has stood up for this person all along, for these people to try to comprehend that this person could do these hellish things to a child is far beyond the realm of their understanding.

Some are ready to forgive and forget, that's fine, please lets wait just a moment. The person has to get help, the pedophile must get therapy, this is a must, otherwise the chances are very high that once the fear factor wares off that the pedophile will be right back to their old behavior.

Yes, love and forgiveness is very important in the healing process, but tough love maybe needed when working with some pedophiles.

Yes there is hope for the pedophile, that once they have continued their therapy, that one can live a very productive life. Yes their sickness can be in remission, but they need to stay away from children. They need to stay in a therapy program that is designed for sex offenders, as well.

Knowing, caring and loving a person that is accused of one of the most horrific things ever, as molesting a child, is unheard of, there is no way that this kind, loving, caring individual could hurt a fly well enough alone a precious child. Hearing of these allegations could enrage some people. The family and friends of this pedophile are hurt, devastated as well. It's ok to give the pedophile love and support, but they must do their time, they must pay for their crime, so their healing process can begin as well.

Trying to rescue the pedophile is not helping them at all. They truly need all the therapy and help that they can get, and freedom, at this early stage, is not the answer at that time.

WHAT HAVE WE LEARNED?

We have learned that pedophilia is a psychological, personality disorder, a learned behavioral sickness, which is a chosen behavior. That could be traced, in most cases, all the way back to the pedophile's childhood/teens. This is not a sickness that all of a sudden one wakes up one day and decides to rape/molest a child. In most cases this behavior has been acted out upon more then one victim before the pedophile is caught.

Pedophilia can be controlled, if the pedophile so chooses, by therapy and that person's choice to have "NO MORE VICTIMS" in their life, of course things are a lot harder then that simple decision, they don't need to be made harder, but the pedophile is the one that makes things difficult.

In some cases the pedophile honestly doesn't see anything that they are doing is really all that bad. Even after all that is being published about how devastating all these things are to the victims, the pedophile can still justify that what they are doing is different and it doesn't harm the children as the TV and papers say. A pedophile has themselves convinced that they truly love the child and they are not hurting this child in any way. This is to justify to them so they may continue to rape/molest the children they choose.

In most cases the pedophile just don't care, they want what they want and they want it right now, and they don't care how they get it, or from what child.

During these times the pedophile has, or chooses to have forgotten all the hell and torment that they went through as a child, all the devastation and nightmares that they went through, to act out as they have on others. How could someone that has been through all of this hell pass it on to others???

Some pedophiles are further acting out their hell, their pain, the anger and rage that is still tearing them apart, the pedophile is choosing to act out and hurt others as they have been hurt, if for nothing else as a temporary relief. That is all the acting out is, but only a temporary relief for the pedophile's pain.

Some pedophiles have not been raped/molested as a child, but choose to molest children for any of a number of reasons.

The pedophile may have gone through a lot of psychological, physical and mental abuse as a child, by their mom, dad, sibling (s), or by some adult in charge of their care. Slowly the child begins to form different kinds of coping skills to try to handle the hell that they are going through. The child may slowly begin to build walls in their minds against males or females, depending on the ones that are harming them the most. The child will do one of two things—want to get closer to the abuser; the closer one is to the abuser the less that they may get hurt, on the other hand, the child may begin to push oneself away because they have been hurt enough. The child begins to try to deaden oneself to all of the pain only to try to cope with this on going hell.

These walls that some pedophiles learn to build will be carried with them into adulthood. The pedophile may believe that the only way that they survived was of all the walls they had built in themselves for coping with this hellish life they had to lead.

Some children go through a lot of psychological abuse. The parent(s), the sibling(s), some family member(s), or other children may make fun of this child a lot for one reason or another. The child may be a slow learner at school, a lot of peers will single this child out and make fun of them, cutting the child down and in some cases are very cruel to this child. Then to have further verbal abuse at home from family is a lot for anyone to try to handle.

As a child grows up and into their teens, maturity is creeping into their lives. When the child is in the seventh or eighth grade they will have P.E. and during shower time some of the other kids make fun of this child because of the way that the child looks, makes fun of their body, and how small that this child is, further laughing and joking is near unbearable for this child.

Then due to all of these things that have happened to this child, and the child further building walls to protect them, they slowly begin to make choices so they will be less hurt.

If the young person is told enough times that there is now way that they will ever be able to satisfy the opposite sex, that they are so ugly that no one will like them, needless to say a child will begin to believe these things, which all adds to their negative self worth and their self esteem.

Then by the time this young adult, now, takes this big chance and finds someone that cares for them, all this garbage that has been drilled into this person is brought into this relationship. Then when that special time comes with this consenting adult, all things that could go wrong during this special moment does, which only confirms all that negative things that people have been saying about them all along. To protect themselves, some young adults will begin to make choices that will devastate many innocent people in the future, if they don't get the help that they need at that time.

Really nothing is wrong with these people, they are people that have gone through a very hellish childhood, they'll be ok, and things will turn out ok—Right????

There are a lot of people that have gone through all kinds of hell as a child and as they grew up they made the right choices, decisions not to hurt others. All Children that have been sexually exploited don't turn out to be pedophiles when they grow up. It is all in the decision making process of the individual, it's all in the choices of that person. This abuse that the person has gone through has or will in someway affect that person's life, it is still suggested to go through therapy to begin to heal the wounds that are still there. The unseen wounds, the wounds that want to be forgotten and left in the past are the wounds that need healing the most. Sometime, somewhere they can sneak up on you and slowly overwhelm you, especially after more and more is being found out about this sickness, and more people are coming forward sharing their horrific stories. The things that has happened to you was not normal, they have affected you in one-way or another, please seek help and healing for these problems. There are enough victims, now is a time for healing.

Most people that are pedophiles have little to nothing to do with homosexuality. These are pedophiles that have the urge to have sex with only children. Then there are homosexuals that have sex with consenting adults of their same sex. These are two totally different kinds of people.

Most are totally against the other; most pedophiles are disgusted with a homosexual's behavior, just as much as a homosexual is disgusted with the pedophile's behaviors. To compare one with the other is the difference between day and night. Even though a male pedophile may have only male victims, this doesn't necessarily make him a homosexual. (The same holds true with female pedophiles as well). They (pedophiles) both have tendencies for the opposite sex, they would love to have sex with the opposite sex (or peer sex), but due to their individual hang-ups they choose to have sex with children for their own selfish reasons. So in most cases when talking of pedophiles, homosexuality is totally different type of people.

Even though we have learned a little more history about pedophilia, doesn't justify that pedophile's devastating behavior at all. No matter how much hell an individual has gone through is no reason to torment, rape/molest another person. So all of these things are knowledge and not justifications for their behavior.

Knowledge is power; knowledge is to be empowering. This knowledge is to be used to help the victims, their families on to the road of the healing process, the same for the pedophiles as well.

CHAPTER II

CYCLE OF BEHAVIORS

As mentioned in the last chapter, that pedophilia is very hard to detect. If one doesn't really know that this behavior maybe going on, it is hard to tell.

The behavior of a pedophile is much like the behavior of a normal caring, loving, kind individual that truly loves and cares for children, and a true desire to help out the families. The big differences are is that the pedophile chooses to use all of that to get closer to the child, to soon wean the child from the family to get more of the child's trust. All of this has one purpose and that is to soon rape/molest the child at the pedophile's whim.

Let's take a look at behaviors, focusing first on the pedophile's behavior. We are going to look at what is called a "3 Stage Cycle".

Stage I: Build-Up

Stage II: Acting Out

Stage III: Aftermath

STAGE I: THE BUILD-UP

Not all, but most pedophiles have a cycle that they go through. Most pedophiles don't just abduct children off the streets then rape/molest them. Most pedophiles are more cunning, conning, manipulative, and premeditative than that. The stalking of the child and all things that the pedophiles ties to this procedure is an extreme high, the pedophile gets lots of hype, some get a huge adrenalin rush.

The pedophile will drive around, or walk around parks, school yards, public swimming pools, neighborhoods, any place they feel will have a lot of children is where they begin their stalking for a potential victims. Most pedophiles are very choosy in the children that they pick. Most don't want the child that seems to be very popular. Most pedophiles will focus on the child that seems to be a loaner. That when seen the child is all alone, the child seems to have little to no friends, the child seems to be very unhappy most of the time. This type of child is the one that most pedophiles will focus on and begin to stalk. (One might say that the pedophile is looking for a child that reminds them a lot of their selves).

Most pedophiles will soon learn the child's name; either by just out right asking the child, or from other children in the area. They will stalk the child to learn where the child lives, the pedophile may also know if the child has any brothers or sisters, if they still have parents. The pedophile will go to great lengths, at times, before they even say "HI" to the child for the first time.

The main idea is to have the child feel as safe as possible, not to scare the child; if the child hears their name, and a person seems to know some things about them, they may feel a little more at ease and not be scared and run off in fear.

Other pedophiles may be involved in all sorts of junior sports like T-Ball, Little League, ice hockey, soccer, etc. Also pedophiles maybe involved in Cub/Boy/Girl Scouts, Big Brother/Sister Programs, teachers to the local clergy.

In any program where the pedophile may find NEEDY children is where they could be at, searching and stalking their potential victim.

Now all of this is to be used as knowledge, for one to be aware of a need to have open and complete communication with your child. This information is not to scare you, or your child, not for you to become a super over-protective parent(s), nor for you to feel the need to smother your child in hopes to protect your child from harm. This extreme could be detrimental to your child as well.

If you have open and complete communication with your child, and if anything does come up, your child will feel free to let you know of anything that has happened to them that has made them feel very, very uncomfortable.

Pedophiles thrive on secrets, when you and your children have "No Secrets", when it comes to things like this, is one of the most important things that will aid in keeping your children safe.

Also, PLEASE keep this in mind as well, that there are many, many people that truly love children and truly want to help children all that they can. There are many of these people out there that are helping children daily. These people are fantastic people and need to be applauded more often.

It's weeding the pedophiles out and away from the children is the task at hand.

That is why it is so important to have this open communication with your children; still it may be hard for your child to share if anything is to happen, they know that you are there and that you will listen to them

when they begin to share—this is so, so important to them.

Once the pedophile has chosen the potential victim that they want, and found out all the things that the pedophile wishes to find out about the child at the time, and then the pedophile will plot and plan for the first contact with the child. The pedophile will have a number of fantasies about this first contact as well.

Soon the pedophile will make the first contact with the child, slowly but surely the pedophile will befriend the child. All along the pedophile will know exactly what to do to make the child feel good, to feel important, to feel special. The pedophile knows what to do to get the child's attention, most all of these things the child may not be getting at home for one reason or another.

Soon the pedophile will make more arrangements to meet the child at a park, playground, and any place where the child may feel relatively safe, just to befriend the child more.

If the child has other brothers and sisters that the pedophile maybe interested in at a later date, the pedophile will befriend them as well.

The next thing that some pedophiles may do is to befriend the rest of the family, the child's mom and dad. The pedophile may try to become an actual part of the family. The family only seeing, or choosing to see the good traits of the pedophile, and the family may have no idea what is up the pedophile's sleeve. All the family is seeing is a kind, loving, and caring person that loves children. These are all things that the pedophile is banking on, and they are going to great lengths to convey.

So when the pedophile has accomplished befriending the family, then they will slowly begin to wean the potential victim more and more away from the family. The pedophile will want the child to be alone with them more and more. They will want the child to stay on over night trips may it be at their place, camping and fishing trips, to short vacation trips only including the potential victim. This will get the potential victim more used to the pedophile, and to trust the pedophile even more. Also during this time there will be genuine caring developing in the child for the pedophile. The child may even begin to love this person, and grow very fond of this person and all the things that the pedophile is doing for the child. Well, maybe this child has never felt this way before; to the child there is someone that appears to love this child, and will do almost anything for the child and will give them almost anything that they want. The pedophile will tell the child how much that they care for and may even tell the child that they love them; that the pedophile would be totally lost without the child, which the child means so much to them. All of this to only get closer to the child and to soon get what they have wanted all along. The pedophile for sometime now has been setting up the child, and their family. The pedophile has now got an investment in the child, maybe even the family. The pedophile has done a lot of things for both, only to claim the payday very soon.

The pedophile has played this acting out scenario in their heads a thousand times already. They have a time, place, and all the things the pedophile wants to happen all planned out in their heads, down to the things that they want the child to say and do.

This is played so much over and over in the pedophile's head that soon that is not enough; the pedophile will soon put the acting out into play.

STAGE II: ACTING OUT

Here is where the pedophile will do everything that they can to get what they have wanted all along.

If the child say NO, or resists in anyway the pedophile will go all out to get what they want. The pedophile may go to begging and pleading of the child. The pedophile will then tell the child how much they truly love the child and that they would do anything in the world for them, that they love the child so much that they want to show their love in this special way. The pedophile will promise the child almost anything to get what they want. If all fails, the pedophile may go, as far as to use threats of hurting the child are someone in their family.

The pedophile will bring up all that they have done for the child and the family and now all they are asking is for this special time with them.

The pedophile will try everything in their power, short of really physically hurting the child (only because they have plans to continue to rape this child later) to get what they want. Sorry to say—most pedophiles will get what they want.

The child may try to run away—to no avail…

The child may try to push the predator away, even start crying, and say NO, NO…The child may try all that they can to stop this rape—to no avail. The predator may stop, (for fear that the child will tell), but the pedophile will do all they can to soften the child up for the next time.

The child may feel nasty, and filthy, along with helpless, confused, betrayed, hurt, and scared to death. In some cases the victim is petrified with fear. The child may act as though they are in a trance, like they may not even be in their body. The victim is so stricken in fear that the only way that they can cope with the moment is to like leave their body. Some victims may talk about like an out of body experience, like they are looking from afar to all of the things that are being done to them, this is so horrible for the victim.

The child, in most cases, don't understand what is happening or why. Total confusion surrounds this whole thing that is happening to them. These things are happening, and this adult is saying how much they care for them, how much that they love the child, and how this adult cannot do without this child, this child means the world to them. When all along this child wants these terrible things to stop and get over with soon so they can get home.

STAGE III: AFTERMATH

Here is where the pedophile will try to make all better with the child. They will begin to tell the child (again) how really special that the child is to them and that is the reason that they done these things, because the pedophile loves the child. The pedophile will beg the child not to tell, that this is his or her special little secret and to NEVER tell anyone about what happened.

The pedophile may tell the child that when two adults love each other they have sex, so there is nothing wrong to what WE did or will do. The adults wouldn't believe them anyway is something else that the pedophile will tell the child.

Anything that the pedophile may have promised the victim before, most pedophiles will pay up, only to keep the child from telling first of all, and to have the child close to them and to keep coming back for the next time.

Most children when they have been raped/molested there will be some kind of behavioral changes, may it be in their attitudes about themselves, a family member, things that normally never really bothered them, may make them nervous or upset now. The child might isolate themselves more, they may choose to stay in their rooms, or stay at home a lot more then before. They may stop hanging out with some of their regular friends, and be around a certain older person more then before.

Really knowing your child well will help them from possible years of exploitation.

If one notices their child to have things that you know that you didn't buy them, and you know that your child never had that kind of money to buy them; one needs to talk with the child to see where the gifts came from and why weren't you told about it before hand? One can do this diplomatically, and lovingly as not to scare the child. All you want is answers, and if things don't seem to add up, then you may need to talk to the person that gave your child these things. Red flags need to be going up in your head, and you may want to watch your child a little more closely.

Please keep in mind to not scare your child, but mainly reassure them that if anything that is happening to them that they don't understand, that the child can talk to them at anytime about anything. Reassure the child that the parent/adult is there for them with any and all problems that they might have at that time.

Keeping those channels of communications open at all times will help. If the child doesn't say anything at first, all one can do is watch and observe the child's behavior.

Parents, these things are not your fault either...

Chances are very high that if the pedophile is not turned in to the proper authorities when there are credible allegations that the pedophile will continue to rape/molest children. Without proper sex offending therapy the chances are extremely high that the pedophile will re-offend.

Even though therapy is not the magic wand, the magic cure, it seems to be the only real avenue that a pedophile has to learn of who they are (good and bad), to learn of the damage and devastation that they have caused, and to truly want to change, because they don't want to devastate no more lives like they have in the past. A good therapy program will help them to do that very thing.

So there is hope for the pedophile, and that one day the pedophile can live a very productive life, with "NO MORE VICTIMS", they can be proud of their achievements, their goals, have a nice job, and live the rest of their lives with little to no trouble. It's all their choice, their decisions, to live right. Which may include some kind of therapy the rest of their lives.

The victims, there is hope all the way, because once they begin to share their horrific nightmares, the hell and torment that they have endured, that power and control that was once over their lives will soon begin to lessen. The more they talk in their groups, and the more that they hear others' stories, all helps in their personal healing process.

So therapy is part of the healing process for both the victim and the pedophile, this is a very important step.

Next, we will be talking about the Beginning Of The Healing Process, and how very important this step is for all...

PART II

THE VICTIMS

THE PRECIOUS INNOCENT DOVES

We have covered a lot of ground and have shared a lot of information with you so far, now is the time to begin to refocus, and lets talk about the victims, and then we will begin to talk about the healing process.

If you are a victim of sexual abuse, physical and/or mental abuse, domestic abuse, it will be very beneficial for you to continue your therapy, if not start a therapy program soon. You are a very special and unique person and you are entitled to live the best life that you can live. If you are letting the past control your life now is the time to begin your change.

It is time for the victims to stand their ground and to be heard, so the beginning of their healing process can begin. This will not be an easy task, but the process can be done, the victims do have the power and control over their lives, and making the decision to get help is the beginning.

The monstrous acts that have happened to you were not your fault. You did not deserve any of these things that happened to you. You were a very special, very precious child only looking for acceptance, love, and understanding. You were not looking for the devastating hell that was bestowed upon you. You were a child/teen that was striving to find yourself in this huge, scary picture called "LIFE". You may have been going through a lot of different things in your life at home, and at school. You may have felt that people did not want you, didn't care for you, maybe you didn't feel loved. You may have never heard the words "I LOVE YOU" from anyone. With all of these things going on you may have been suffering from very low self worth and self-esteem.

Then comes a person in your life with all the things that you felt that you never had, this person tells you just how special and how great that you are, and they seem to take an interest in you and all the things that you do. Each and every day this person is there giving you compliments and support. This person has befriended others in your family too; the family seems to really like this person too.

This nice person begins to want to be alone with you more and more. You are alone at their place, they may take you to the stores, to the movies, maybe camping and fishing, and you are beginning to like this person a lot. They seem to be a little touchy, feely at times which makes you a little uncomfortable, but they like you right, someone that likes you does get close to you—right???

Then this person is buying you different things, taking you out to eat, buying you clothes for school, and you may even get to go on some vacations with this person. Then this person wants you to stay over night at their place…This is when the horror, the hell begins.

See, none of these things that followed were your fault, YOU were a sweet, innocent, loving child wanting all the love and attention that you could get (any child would be that way), then the monster part of this person came out and devastated your life. Oh how you wanted all those things to end.

Will all those things can end!!!

You can take complete and total control of your life, maybe for the first time. You don't have to give the past control over you any longer.

"Today is the first day of the rest of your life; take control of it, embrace it, be happy and rejoice in it. Life is to short to let the pasts have control YOU TAKE CONTROL live your life to the fullest you deserve that!!!!!!

I know that some of us may not believe some of the things above, please keep reading, it only gets better.

You are a very special human being that has been through a hellish torment; it's now time to take control of our lives again so we can live the best that we can for now on and into our future. Things will not be easy, but we can work together and you may seek a therapy program for you so you can begin/or continue your "HEALING PROCESS".

It's never too late to begin/ or continue your therapy program, your mental health is so important to you, to your family and to the people that know you.

YOU ARE VERY SPECIAL, UNIQUE, AND A CARING AND LOVING HUMAN BEING, YOU DESERVE TO LIVE YOUR LIFE TO THE BEST THAT YOU CAN, TAKE CONTROL OF YOUR FUTURE TODAY!!!!

CHAPTER III

BEGINNING THE HEALING PROCESS

The victims of sexual abuse, physical/mental abuse, domestic violence, other types of abuse/violence may choose to go through a healing process, so one day these victims may love their selves once again and begin to live the best lives that they can possibly choose to live.

These victims have gone through maybe years of abuse, hell, torture, unmentionable nightmares, maybe total and complete destruction of their self worth and self-esteem.

Some of the victims may still think that what has happened to them must have been their fault; that they have caused this hell that has fallen upon them. If it wasn't for something that they had done, or said, all of these things

67

would not of happened to them. Their predator(s), I'm sure have told them these same things.

Most of the victims have gone through so much indescribable torment, and hell that they just want to do their best to live their lives. These devastating acts, to some victims, are so horrific that the victim don't want to bring them up any more. They want to forget these things, and want to act, as they never, ever happened, so they can go on living their lives the best that they can.

There is so many reasons that a victim may have to not begin their healing process; to not seek out therapy, here too the reasons may near endless.

This book is not to force anyone to do anything that they don't want to do, because therapy will only work if one will let it. This book is wanting to let one know that you are a very <u>precious</u> <u>human</u> <u>being</u>, that you deserve

the best that life can offer, and maybe working through these past horrific events can set one more free and onto the road further in their healing process.

Do you believe that you are a very precious human being????

Do you believe that you deserve the best that life has to offer???

If you answered "NO" to either question, you may choose to seek therapy to help you work through the hell that continues to affect you to this day.

Some victims will have a number of reasons as not to dig up this past; the predator(s) are not in their lives no more; the predator(s) is dead or a thousand miles away from them. All of these and more things will a victim say, when their healing process is just a call away.

This healing process will not be an easy road for most, because bringing those old nightmares, all that hell that they had went through, can be very over-whelming once again. Some can understand the reasons why a lot of victims choose not to go back there again.

A few things to continue to keep in mind are:

That the things that happened to you were not your fault. You were and innocent, and very precious human being in all of that hell and torment. Truly believe this...

You did not deserve any of the terrible things that happened to you. No human being deserves to be treated as you were treated. Learn to believe this...

Continually tell yourself that you are a very precious, special human being, and you deserve the best that your life has to offer. *Please learn to believe this!!!*

You want to learn how to love your self again. You want to have your self worth and your self -esteem back, strong and intact. You would love to have that gleam back in your eyes, that happiness back inside you, you would love to have your spirit free and alive inside you once again.

You want your inner child, who may be frozen at the age of your first abuse, to know and understand that you love them, that things are ok or will be ok, and nothing was their fault; that you will learn to protect that inner child, so that they will never be hurt again. That you will be listening to their cries, and that the both of you will be going through this healing process together.

It's ok to trust people that truly love you, that truly care for you, and want to help you. That there are a lot of people that want to help you through the hell and torment, and to reassure you that there is a light at the end of the tunnel.

The only way to get there is to walk through this darkness of the past; being reassured that you are not taking this journey by yourself this time. That there are people around you that have went through similar tragedies and want to help you in your healing process, almost as much as you.

One way of fully living your life in freedom and in the light is to confront the darkness of the past. Talk about and share all the things that have happened in that darkness. Stop giving your past any power over your life at all, that was then and now is now. You have the total power now, you have total control over your life and your future, you can handle this power very well, be confident, be assertive, and you will succeed.

You are more precious than all the gold in the universe. There is only one special person like you in this entire galaxy; you are more precious then all the diamonds in the entire universe. You are very unique, and a very valuable person, and no one could EVER replace you even if they tried. (A clone would not ever come close to you). You are precious and as delicate as a snowflake, but you are a survivor and you are as strong and as bold as the highest mountains.

That's right, YOU are a survivor and you will refuse to be a victim any longer, you can choose to begin your healing process at anytime.

A nice program to search for may be able to offer you some one-on-one counseling, plus have a group or groups that you may choose from.

One of the hardest things to find is a nice therapy plan you can afford. Even though you are worth the best, most cannot afford it. So you must choose the best that you can afford at that time.

You must tell yourself that you deserve this special treatment, you deserve these groups to aide in your healing process, you deserve to be as healthy of a person as you can be, this therapy will help you to achieve this goal of yours, if you allow it.

You'll need to take things slow and easy. You did not come this far through all of your hell and torment over night, so your healing process will not be done over night or just a few meetings either. Your healing process will begin when you make that decision, and your healing process will end when you feel that you have accomplished all that you can possibly resolve at that time. YOU have the POWER...

So if your healing process takes quit awhile, that doesn't make you a bad person, you are using your group(s) to the best that you can to help you to become even a better person then you are already. So take your time and don't base your recovery, or your wellness according to someone else. *You are very special and very unique; believe this in your heart of hearts!!!*

Being in a group setting will help you more then one can imagine. There you will be able to see that there are others that have similar problems as you. You will see that you are not the "Lone Ranger" here, and you will see and hear how some of these people are on the road to becoming survivors, just like you are striving for at that time.

Caution!!! Some of these people have gone through some very horrific and very devastating lives, just as you have in your time. In some cases you may think that these people have gone through more hell then you ever did, and you begin to question yourself why are you there in this group, you have never experienced anything like these people have in their lives. Please stop yourself from these thoughts…You are all victims of a horrific abuse or you would not be in that group. Your horrific experiences and all the hell that you went through was very traumatic to you—and those are the issues to be looked at—the issues in each and every person in the group. So what someone has gone through is just as horrific as what you went through—to you. Keep in mind your uniqueness…

See these people are tired of giving their past that power and control over almost all parts of their lives.

These people are tired of having one of their precious love ones to touch them in a special way, and they may react in a panic, fear may begin to rip through their entire body, and they may not understand why!!!!

You and your special love one may be trying to work through a problem that has arrived in your lives; this person may say something in a certain way that you choose to be triggered to some past happening, you may become violently upset, begin to tremble, and want to fight this person away. Later you or your love one do not understand why this violent behavior.

These people want to enjoy themselves and their love ones to the fullest. They want to enjoy being held, cuddled, and are able to lay next to their special someone and not feel dirty, filthy, nasty, nor tremble in fear and shame. All of this will take time.

A lot of which can be received by simply making a decision to work through the darkness of the past, so one day you can live in the loving warmth of the light.

Some of your healing process can begin by sharing some of your past with your love one(s), sharing with a very special friend that you truly trust and care for, that will respect you and your feelings. All of which is a very important beginning for you. Then you will still need to get some professional help as in a group setting and one on one therapy as well, to help you through this very special journey that you will soon choose to take.

REMEMBER: *That you are very special, you are very unique, and you deserve the best life that you can possibly have—you have the total and complete power to make this*

new life happen. Begin by working through the darkness of your past, and into the light of your bright new future…

Once you have worked on a number of issues in your past and have a good since of self worth and self-esteem, you are beginning to feel like you are taking more control over your life and you have a since of self confidence. You are beginning to love yourself, and are more forgiving of yourself and the things that have happened to you. You have put the blame of the devastating things in your life where they belong, and you can see your innocence in all of the torment.

You have walked through most of the darkness of your past and you are beginning to feel the warmth of the light just in front of your future. There is love and happiness in your heart that hasn't been there, to this degree, for as long as you can remember.

You are happy, your inner child is happy, your loved ones are extremely happy for you, as your friends are all rejoicing in your healthier life you have chose to take.

You can fully rejoice in all of your accomplishments, you have done a fantastic job, and I'm sure you must feel like a new person almost.

All of this is very great, our journey is not over yet, and we still have a few hills and valleys to go through yet.

During our journeys we have went through in our past we may still have some resentments, some lingering anger, maybe hatred of the horrific things that have happened to you—all fully understandable I assure you. This next chapter is also very vital to our healing process, and this may very well be just as hard to do as all that you have accomplished up to this point.

The Forgiveness Process is very empowering to you, this whole process is for you and for no one else; your past is inside of you and no one else. You are a different person now and you have worked through a lot of things in your past. You feel stronger about your self then you ever have before, this is just another step of letting go of the past that has bound you for so long.

Take this process only when you are ready, you may have to take it a couple of times to resolve all that needs to be resolved in this process, but you can do it, and you will soon see why it is so important to go through.

CHAPTER IV

THE FORGIVENESS PROCESS

I'm sensing some anxiety, some tension, maybe even some anger over the possibility of forgiving one's predator(s) for the hell that they have put you through. All of which is fully understandable, all I ask is to hear me out, because this could be a very important part of your healing process. This may help you to put the closure that you are so searching for, and may help you to a fuller, richer life with yourself...

*No one is asking you to forget all those horrid things that have happened to you—NO.

*No one is saying that when you choose to forgive, that means letting the predator(s) off the hook, that the predator(s) is free and clear, as nothing happened—

NO...The predator needs to serve the time for their crime.

*No one is saying that in order to achieve your full healing process that you Must forgive your predator(s). Not at all...

This forgiveness process is not for the predator(s) at all, but just one more step to look at to help put more closure to your past hell. It's an empowering tool for YOU!

Once you have talked about a lot of the past nightmares, sharing the hell, torment, and at times the debilitating horror, pain and anguish, you are beginning to give less and less power to these things in the past. The more and more these monstrous things are brought to light, the less and less monstrous they will soon become. By no means does that mean that they did not happen, by no means does that discount any of your thoughts and feelings about these things. That this could be a sign that you are taking control of your life even more now and it's time to move on in our healing journey.

Keep in mind that we are talking about you and your mental and physical well being and that these things are only suggestions to help you to try to achieve to be the best person that you can be, nothing else. You must make the choices to what is best for you and when.

In this "forgiveness process", we are going to look at resentments, which fuels anger, hate, and negative behavior.

The victim has every right to their thoughts and feelings about their predator(s), and all the things that have happened to them. No one has the right to try to take that away from the victim.

How does the victim think when they hold onto all those thoughts of the past and to all the things that has happened to them? They have negative, angry, rage full, resentful, retaliatory thoughts, which lead to how the feel not only about the predator(s), but also negative feelings about themselves as well. All of which could soon lead to very devastating behavior, if the victim doesn't defuse these thoughts and negative feelings soon. In essence, we are giving the predator(s) more control over our lives. This predator(s) maybe dead, or they may be thousands of miles away from the victim. The predator(s) may not have seen the victim in decades, as long as the victim chooses to let the past to continue to invade their lives, they are giving this predator(s) more power, which is what happens when we choose to hold onto our resentments of the past.

There will come a time in our healing process, at that individual victim's time that they may choose this forgiveness process. In order for this process to be effective the victim must be willing and ready to begin, understanding that there will be some victims that will never choose to go this far in their therapy; the victim may not be able to forgive this predator(s); the victim may not really understand what is to be achieved by wanting to go through this process. We all know that this process is not going to be easy—none of what the victim has endured has been easy. The victim will need to focus on that this forgiveness is for their mental state of mind and not for the predator(s).

As a for instance:

A victim has very deep hatred, rage, and resentments towards their father. This person has done unmentionable devastation to the victim for years. There was even times when the victim really wanted to harm, even kill their father, hoping that would end the predator's reign of hell and torment over their lives. The victim even had thoughts of suicide; their pain was so great.

Finally there was a very stormy divorce in the process, where even more hell and havoc rained out over the entire family. The nightmares and torment continued long after the father was taken out of the house, he was forbidden to come anywhere close to this family. The father soon moved miles away from this family...Years later the nightmares still plagued the victim. The victim would wake up in cold sweats, extremely angry, rage full, cussing and gnashing their teeth, begging and pleading for all of these nightmares to stop, to end. This victim is allowing their predator to continue to have power and control over their lives, thousands of miles away from them.

Again, it is fully understandable why the victim is going through all of this hell. We do not want to take

away anything from the pain that the victim is going through, not at all. All of this is genuine and understandable.

The victim's anger, rage, and resentments are now eating the victim alive, which is also understandable, because the victim doesn't know what to do to get rid of all of this unbearable pain.

The victim can come to terms with all of these resentments, and for the victim, one day, to soon forgive their predator for all the hell that they caused them, to truly forgive the predator, for the victim's healing, for the victim's peace of mind.

SUGGESTION:

A way one might do this is to one day sit down and make a list of all the things that angers the victim, which upsets the victim about their predator. May a list be of one thing or a hundred—a thousand and one things, it's the victim's list and one else's.

Then for the victim's forgiveness process, the victim will look over the list, and at the victim's pace, the victim will one by one truly forgive the predator(s) of everything on their list. Once something is truly forgiven, lets not pick that thing up and harbor all the anger and rage behind it again. One needs to check themselves, "Oh, I have forgiven this person of this", admit what you have done to yourself, check your thoughts and feeling, ok now let's move on in our healing process.

This process may be a long and very emotional roller coaster ride for the victims, all of which is a part of their healing process, if they make the choice or not.

"THE FORGIVENESS PROCESS IS FOR THE VICTIM, AND THE VICTIM'S

MENTAL HEALTH, AND FOR NO OTHER REASONS"...THIS IS VICTIM EMPOWERMENT...

Letting that victim know they have that power, that total and complete power over their decision making process, that power over their lives will mean so much to that victim.

So lets say that you have gone through your total healing process, you went through your forgiveness process, with some delays, but you understand what was to be accomplished in that process and you achieved it.

Some of us feel fantastic to finally once and for all to get our lives back under OUR control. That doesn't mean that we don't run across some problems in our lives, but now we have new purpose and new meaning. We are survivors, we have concurred the beast, and we will get through these shortfalls.

Some of us might still fill empty for some reason, that there is something missing in our lives now and we can't quite put our finger on it.

There may be a hole where we once had all this anger, hatred, rage and resentments for the predator(s). This hole now needs to be filled with positive, good, fantastic things about yourself and the people now in you life that love you and have stood faithfully beside us all these years and through our healing process.

*Do not leave these holes vacant for long, but fill them with kind, and loving things about yourself and your love ones...*Pat these thoughts firmly in your mind, all of which will soon round off your healing process.

You will soon choose to make a lot of very important changes in your life on your road of the "Healing Process". You will be climbing mountains and concurring problems that you have never thought possible before in your life. There will come a time where you will see how important this "Forgiveness Process" is in your healing. You will slowly make that decision—on your own—to go through this process—FOR YOU!!!! All of which is fantastic, and great, how proud you need to be of yourself and all that you have accomplished.

We have one more bridge to cross, we have one more person to forgive, one more person to love like we have never loved before...

THIS PERSON—IS—YOU!!!!!!

There is only one person that has gone through your hell and torment in your shoes. There is only one person that has gone through your devastation, humiliation, agony, and pain. Then this day you have made the choices to take total and complete control of your life once again, and after all that one has been through is now a SURVIVOR, strong and true.

Now that you have, or soon will be, going through your healing process in a group of your choosing, you know and believe that all the things that happened to you were not your fault. There was nothing that you did to cause anything that happened to you. You were a precious human being then as you are still until this day. You didn't deserve nor did you ask for all the hell that rained over you.

"DO YOU LOVE YOURSELF????" "DO YOU CARE FOR AND LOVE YOURSELF, AS YOU HAVE NEVER DONE BEFORE IN YOUR LIFE????

After all that you have been through, after all you have or will soon accomplish, LOVING YOURSELF will be the icing on the cake of your recovery.

WE MUST REMEMBER <u>ALWAYS</u>, WHAT HAPPENED TO US WAS NOT OUR FAULT, THESE THINGS WERE NOT GOD'S FAULT, BUT HUMAN KINDS FAULT. Some humans have that tendency to want to devastate others at times, which is very wrong and all things need to be told to responsible people so you and other victims can get the help that is needed for your healing.

WHAT IS DONE IN DARKNESS <u>MUST BE</u> BROUGHT TO LIGHT!!!

The victims of sexual abuse, of domestic violence, mental and physical abuse, you don't need to stand for that hell these people are putting you and your family through. Stand you're ground, make your voice heard, all of this hell that is done in darkness, empower yourself, help bring these things to light. Fight to become a survivor and don't remain a victim any longer.

There are people and places out there that truly want to help you and to help you with your healing process, ask, reach out, and search for the group and plan that is best for YOU. You have been a victim for way to long—

LOVE YOURSELF!!

BECOME A SURVIVOR!!!!

The "Forgiveness Process" was very hard for me as well, when I first heard about "Forgiveness", I said that there was no way in creation that I was going to forgive the ones that aided in devastating my life at that point. I was near furious of just thinking that someone would imply that I should forgive these people.

After that initial response, and I settled down—a lot—I began to listen instead of reacting.

I was not going through this process of "forgiveness" for the predators in my life, put to give me the choice to begin to resolve some of my resentments that I have against these people (and rightfully so, no one has ever said that I should not be anger about the things that have happened to me). When I began resolving some of these resentments that I had more and more of my anger, hatred, and rage slowly began to lift about the things that surrounded my past. I slowly became more and more relieved, feeling less oppressed, happier in my everyday life. The more and more that I worked in the area of "forgiveness" the better that I felt.

See I wasn't letting no one off the hook for all of those things that were done to me, I was taking care of myself, resolving these "resentments", which were chains, that I allowed, holding me to the hell and torment of my past. With the help of my spiritual beliefs, and with counseling staff I am here today, a SURVIVOR just like you, or you can be soon.

I went through years of hating myself and have had many suicidal thoughts in my past. I felt that the whole world was against me and that everything bad that ever happened to me was because I must have deserved it, or it wouldn't of happen to me—Right??

WRONG!!!! Today I LOVE myself, I have my self worth and self-esteem back stronger then it ever has been before. I have gone through my "Forgiveness Process", and I truly love myself for this major accomplishment.

At times I still go through some low times, I feel down and depressed, I might begin to revert to some old tapes of my past, but I stop myself. I remind myself of all of my accomplishments, all of the major resolving that I have done, then most of all I tell myself that "I Love You", and I may even give myself a hug, if I need it, and I go one with my life.

Remember to Love Yourself—Become a Survivor!!!

I hope and pray that you choose, or will soon choose to begin your healing process.

You are so precious, so special, you deserve the best life has to offer…Make the choice to stop letting your past control you and your life today. YOU, your family and friends deserve to see the happiness in your life again.

You deserve to see that twinkle in your eyes again…

MAY GOD BLESS YOU AND YOUR FAMILY!!!

IN CLOSING

THE PARADOXICAL PHENOMENON

We have much more knowledge about the beast (pedophilia) then we ever had before. More and more victims, soon survivors, are coming forth and sharing their hell and torment that they have been keeping in the depths of their being for so long.

This beast has had control of the lives of the victims for way to long, it's now time for the victims to reclaim their lives, continue to bring to light all of the hell that was in darkness, and the victims declare their victory, and self-empowerment.

This beast, this monster—is only a part of the pedophile. The monster can be controlled, if the pedophile so wishes. The pedophile needs therapy as well, because they are not strong enough to make the right decisions in the beginning of their therapy.

The pedophile needs to do their time for their crime(s); they need therapy to help them want to change, so when they are released there is a less of a chance of the pedophile of having further victims.

There has been enough hell, torment, devastation and pain; the violence must stop, therapy sought, where new life can begin.

By the victim coming forth sharing their hellish experiences, plus seeking help;

By the pedophile being arrested and sent to a prison that will offer them therapy, will aide in their recovery, if they so choose;

There is hope, and healing for all concerned which is this beautiful "PARADOXICAL PHENOMENON" of this whole road to the Healing Process.

Which leads to positive lives for all concerned...

There is HOPE, there is LOVE, and recovery for all; it's time that we stop letting our past control our lives, and for us to take back that power and control for a better and fuller lives that we have ever had before.

MAY GOD BLESS US ALL!!!!!!!!

Shawn Michael Dove

DEDICATIONS

I want to dedicate this book, first of all, to all of the victims that I have in my life, and to their families as well. No one deserves that hell and torment that I sent these people through. All of these people are in my prayers every night. May God Bless them all!!!

Also I would like to dedicate this book to all victims of sexual abuse, domestic violence, mental and physical abuse, and to give ALL the encouragement to seek help and to share so they can get on or to continue on their road of their "Healing Process".

To let you ALL know that what had happened to you was not your fault, and you did not deserve anything that has happened to you. That you all are very

precious human beings and that you deserve the best your life can offer you...

Last but not least, I want to dedicate this book to my caring and loving family that I love and care for so deeply. I have gone through my "Forgiveness Process" on my father (God rest his soul), and mother, and I love both of my parents with all my heart. They loved me, and stood by me throughout the years, the sign of love and devotion. May God Bless my entire Family!!!!

ACKNOWLEDGEMENTS

First, I want to acknowledge my Heavenly Father for encouraging me to write this book for all the people concerned. I want to thank my Heavenly Father for all of the blessings that I was encouraged to write and to share. It was very difficult at times to share some of these deep and emotional things that I needed to share with people. With the help of the Lord, I was able to share what I needed to share in this book.

I want to acknowledge all of the counseling staff that I was blessed with during my time in prison. I thank each and every one of them for all of their true dedication, and encouragement in my recovery process. I thank and I care for each and everyone that has helped me and others on my road to finding out that damage and devastation that I have caused, and to show me that as long as I care for and love myself, how can I hurt others. Thank you for all of your help.

I also wish to acknowledge the counseling staff that is helping me in my current therapy program, and to continuing to encourage me to be the best that I can be in my today's journeys.

I thank God for all those people that are truly helping others to be the best that they can be...

ABOUT THE AUTHOR

Shawn Michael Dove was born in a small town about and hour or two hours South of Springfield, Illinois, in 1951, just after W.W. II, and during the "Baby Boomers".

Shawn's mother and father loved each other very much. Shawn is the only son of three children, he has two beautiful sisters, younger then him, that he loves deeply to this day.

Even though Shawn's mother and father loved each other a lot problems that couldn't be resolved in this union ended in a divorce when Shawn was only 8 years old. Shawn was totally devastated at that time; he thought that he was the only child in the whole world without a father.

Shawn had a very stormy childhood, where he had developed a lot of issues about women, his sexual orientation, went through a lot of mental, physical, and psychological abuse, and he grew up to be a very confused, and disillusioned, and angry young man.

With all of his hang-ups and confusions about life, he felt the most comfortable to have sex with children, which he began abusing when he was about 12 years old.

In 1990 Shawn was sent to prison for help, he went into a sex offending group and worked hard to change his life for the better. He stayed in the program the entire ten years, and he changed his life remarkably. He understands and sees some of the damage, hell, and horrific pain that he has caused and he doesn't want to harm another human being like that again.

Shawn has learned a lot during his time, and he is sharing his heart in this book with you today. This is just a small part of Shawn wanting to help people that have been afflicted by a pedophile, and reassuring the victims that there is hope, hope in their healing process, and there is life in being a Survivor and not a victim.

Truly,

Shawn Michel Dove